Gallery Books
Editor: Peter Fallon

CAPTAIN LAVENDER

Medbh McGuckian

CAPTAIN LAVENDER

Gallery Books

Captain Lavender
is first published
simultaneously in paperback
and in a clothbound edition
on 30 November 1994.

The Gallery Press
Loughcrew
Oldcastle
County Meath
Ireland

ISBN 1 85235 141 1 (*paperback*)
     1 85235 142 X (*clothbound*)

The Gallery Press receives financial assistance from An Chomhairle
Ealaíon / The Arts Council, Ireland, and acknowledges also the assis-
tance of the Arts Council of Northern Ireland in the publication of this
book.

Contents

'I have not painted the war . . . but I have no doubt that the war is in . . . these paintings I have done.'

— Picasso, 1944

*for my sister Dorothy
and for Sophia Hillan King*

PART ONE

Lines for Thanksgiving

Two floors, their invisible staircase
crouching muscularly,
an old wall, unusually high,
interwoven like the materials for a nest,
the airtight sensation of slates:
all as gracefully apart
as a calvary from a crib
or the woman born in my sleep
from the stranger me that is satisfied
by any street with the solemn name of a saint.

The moon there, fuller than any other,
slips through my fingers into every fold
of the sky in turn, stirring up satin
like a mother roughing a boy's hair.
Eternally repeating its double journey
and the same message, as if it were
still impossible to speak
from one town to the next.

The fire keeping in all night
is an extra gas jet, its several
thicknesses unequal in length
like the rays of a monstrance.
If I had just won a victory
it was over everything that was not
myself, by the water's edge.

Porcelain Bells

for my mother

1 *Candles at Three Thirty*

The year fades without ripening,
but glitters as it withers
like an orange stuck with cloves
or Christmas clouds.

Bits of very new,
dream-quilted sky
are touched to an arrangement,
all but kiss.

Dark blue gathers around the waist
into a humbler colour;
two cottages flush with the road
slowly edge back.

When I am all harbour, ask too much,
go up like the land
to points and precipices,
meanwhile is my anchor.

The island with its quick primrose light
turns aside and walks away
from my swollen shadows,
but carries the road southwards.

Frail as tobacco flowers,
a featherweight seagull
still damp on my brocade curtain
is ready for sea again.

A meaningless white thread
of pale travel-sleep
rippling one side only
of his unlighted eyes,

intelligent and soulless,
sees everybody happening
as down a warmed room.
The upper half of the house made fast,

we try to batten the door-windows,
but one won't fasten,
the thin edge of the sea's blade
curves around its oak, rustless as flesh.

Out between the rosemary hedges,
sky and sea part in a long
mauve-silver tress
like an oyster shell

that has held life between its lips
so long,
it seems so long
since life left it wrecked there.

Winter's frosty standstill
will just leave the lips clear
as on a bridge
of would-be sunshine.

But now the intensification
of light in the lower sky
like a stairway outside
the side of a house

acts directly on the blood,
not the mind, to make the sea
appear more light than water,
familiar as a fireside.

2 *Story Between Two Notes*

You are the story I can't write.
Every page of you
has to be torn out of me.
Even after your death when you are alone
your mysteriously-suppressed
name-sickness
will weave itself into all I see.

It is as if you already listen
from the adjoining room, earthly wagon
harnessed to unearthly horses;
the red years have just failed
to take you out of the world
which looks like another world.

We sit in chairs in faraway countries,
like perfumes that have long since evaporated
complaining of being a memory.
We try to slip through the quarrel
like stowaways.

The only movement I am sure of
is that the fields are bare,
and at the dark climax of September
it requires but one sleep

for the ghostly art of the sea
to clothe his own deep trouble
up the white staircase.

Nobody has ever seen
the true shape of your lips.
You are walled round, a too-well-laid-out path.
You detour round the language
like a wound closing wearily.

But now, when this music is playing between us,
though I never dream meaning into it,
this winter-quiet that loses itself
completely in sound seems the active beginning
of a normal, if still secret, name.

And having filled this word entirely
with yourself, it judges you,
sets fire to you to resuscitate you.
There will of course be no further reference
to it: but the sound missing my ear
is that of the silence of your heart.

3 Speaking into the Candles

This death you have nourished is too orderly,
its fragrance too convincing.
You wear it like an unusually free veil,
so light it flies by me;
the mirror hardly believes it.
Or as if you were living in another town,
rejoining us with a completely different
handwriting, timid and beautiful.

Leaving the room, you break off a piece of the world,
around which my life is standing,
through which my blood spreads.
Missing so much world,
you still hold out your hands for more world,
your footsteps softening like a creature
before whom doors give way.
You lie alone on a new surface,
sharp as your own edge or a strange birthday,
unsleeping early in a new darkness,
too-awake like a brightly lit house,
its prolonged and counted light.
There is a closeness of many lights in you,
like stars moving forward meaningfully.
Every flower in you is everywhere.
Even if you were outside, where summer was,
you would still be inside every leaf.
Pain opens your hands like a book
or a two-syllable word I find as unintelligible
as the windows of other people.
Yet you are continually understanding it,
though now you are drained of all meaning,
and out of politeness try to remember
how to be completely afraid.
What do you care if I, your younger mouth,
stay or leave, though your dress shone upon me
when it willed me into existence?
You cannot anymore be the blue
in my eyes. What is the year to you
when you have moved outside yourself
and endure the motion of the earth
as not being right for you,
growing dark everywhere inside you
as if your air had been driven out
far above you?

Yet even as you refuse to be understood,
like your city in which nothing
is ever forgiven, if I dare
upon your silence, you cry it out whole,
with a full, upward glance,
like a nightingale.
I will survive this late-speaking love
when morning becomes conscious
it is no longer possible —
when the eternal procession of the sky
passes over it as over nature.
It will not be the night
between yesterday and today,
but these less shaken days
I would hold like a resurrection
to my breath.
When you find your way out
of the jewel-groove of your limbs
and the used-up breeze goes past
your icy eyelid,
already no longer anyone's,
I will dive you back to earth
and pull it up with you.

The Appropriate Moment

for Derek Mahon

1 *Faith*

In a mirror stretched across one wall
the front view of you is strong and still.
Then, as though it were my gaze that caused it,
I see you glint along a real pavement.

You give me your mouth uncluttered
by ordinary corrupt human love,
which is like listening to music;
we go the winter walk, the street
flows in your veins, the wilted leaves turn sour
at being the last leaves for many:
it is unmistakably Sunday.

You are thinking and you are not thinking.
Calling all flowers bluebells,
you think you have left time behind on the coast.
Let it out of a window like a sparrow.
But will the sea be outside the window?
Time slips quietly into the place left for it;
the silence in your corner is no deeper.

I could almost tear your voice,
such a dry, old-paper feel to it
like thawing ice or dry straw.
I push it up to the surface
where we are walking round the raised rim
of a lake, the water becoming
the colour of this page.

And the secret of this tint
is the bluish shadow of a great bird
swooping like a mother dream
or a soul who has gone ahead,
a border design of faded red pheasants.

You are giving the name of islands
to the wave of onrushing clouds,
your words as immobile as the moon
in this final race with the unbeautiful dark
I tend to worship.

I read the dark you by matchlight;
you survive into the one flesh
of my received dreams, shapelessly,
a whisper above a lawn, a stretch of wall.

2 *Et Animum Dimittit*

The transparency of his eyes
as he leant backwards to steer
his swaying soul was rain.
In what company
tormentingly sharp rain floundering,
all day a vertical wall
beating the strange earth.

His magnificent photography,
storm after storm, had cut down
the trees on either side of the road.
Even in the bonhomie of morning,
all the voices were turned low
like lamp flames, his own burned
in an ashtray on the bar.

They had lain down, absolute
inseparables, their higher and lower
nature, unwashed, as if their bones
were nothing. They were continually
getting up in darkness as
a great inflated olive moon
worked its lust on their spirits.

His tongue was cramped into a few
very pale, casual sensations
though a thousand years of breeding
moved the bright muscle of his mouth.
The coat that harshly stroked his breast
lay orphaned like a dagger
they had not noticed.

Wayward as generosity, soundlessly
flying, like a loving omniscience
it struck him in the back:
as if he could forget so soon
the finer taste, the finer terror,
of that mute province we call home,
in the sense that we know home.

3 *Astral Picture*

I love to live in afternoon
because of its mysterious stairs.
I love the out of the fog and into the fog
of taxis at midnight with their crumbly
half-kisses, silk sliding back on rings.

They say that I am not I,
but some kind of we, that I do not know

where I end. Sometimes there is no one
to ask, no home for my hand.
I feel my body poured into all the seasons.
I put my hand into a flower
like something with cold blood.

Do you see an action in that,
in your general thirsting after death?
Do you want to separate yourself
from the bird wallpaper of the sunset
that lasts so many hours,
from the cruel sixties
of the numbered houses?
Bits of you remain
whatever gate you go through.

You laugh, as if there were no suddenly
or suddenlys are familiar to you,
like a word that helps you struggle,
but suddenly it seems to me
that there is no such word.

When we meet on the platform
like letters thought and written on a train
or night telegrams, you slip a petal
from some flower into my searching hand,
with the circular moulding of fruit.
You pawn yourself into inverted commas
and kiss dryly.

Everything that can sparkle
does, but one would have expected
the promise to go away by itself
as a circle widens into a swarm of lace:
I still have to grow into your face.

4 *Ignotas in Artes*

Lips applied to other lips,
fingers thrust into fingers, fingers
pulled apart, legs forming angles:
love was the last thing
this surprisingly romantic
fist on the barred door could resemble.

A play of silver on a quilted settee,
outlines of small tables taking shape
in an unbroken, ray-reflecting mirror
that did away with the possibility
of other conversations — the last gold
and last crimson of the garden.

Pitiless as sunset, an enfilade
of light-coloured rooms (flashes
not exactly of beauty but of consciousness)
began slowly advancing out of the dust
in a bloody cloud, but seemed
somehow armless, as if there would be no sunset.

There are evenings that conspire
for happiness, however trivial
and flippant the stars.
There are evenings that long to stay the night,
that hardly sleep because of hope,
because a man spoke every way in vain.

Death on the small scale
of a marine insect, you don't complain,
but this body-breaking journey
was the leap of a torn-out heart

decaying, locked and magical,
into untenanted, uninhabitable space.

When from the plane the miniature river
dropped away like a semi-embrace
and we climbed in long spirals,
sitting square, talking
with immense satisfaction of death,
and a strong sense of being watched,

not only if but also since
Mass without the Sanctus bell
still gives this world back
to its Creator, as the light
went on, I felt myself
among the population of heaven.

The Silkwinder

for Bob Welch

Amazingly visible, often with only
a Tuesday to guide her, time passes
like a wedding morning, promising
many mornings, proper days
and sleep-drenched nights.

The heart stays blooded
with summer seeds, as the trees
which I always think of as bare
bubble up to a pool in my mind
in which the forgiving leaves
slowly exchange their line-pattern
and relics of flowers wind a wristlet
around the impression of a perfect rose.

For about six hours I should make
one of my little addings up of days,
how for six days those leaves flew past
incessantly, in very quick rivers,
till several graves were under leaf,
and my images all of the depths
of the sea, or seaside places.

The amber landscape in the small bedroom
became a small raw spot between wrist
and elbow I touched
each time I came into it,
the excessive sweetness of the pink paper
brought it all back.

I began to conceive of the room as a whole
in relation to the picture

of the silver vase and long flower
from the dining-room:
how the flower was folded up
inside its lip, then came loose,
like waking wider, leaving the inner arm
as dark as it was before.

Unused Water

for Joan McBreen

Lost earrings,
a dash of acrid green
in the wrong time of the year.

How can they have ripened
in the irreflecting night,
they died so thin and hawk-coloured,
like matching clouds, one drying rapidly,
one completely dry.

One letter's opening endearment,
like August's, only gentler,
slips a transparent skin
over the eye just awake
Autumn had left uncored,
as when you put down with the telephone
the whole Atlantic.

Cupboard with Painted Ship

The flowers I picked were a bloodstream
I was standing in. Within the white moment
of the snow going the bomb
brewed unburst in the rosebed.

One month of rare and inky graves
has added nothing. I learned to halve
my rainbeaten bedroom
in that evening-beach colour

was to comb out the sea
like a field of silk scarves
from an eaten nut.
But being unused

the spring necklace
you are just letting curl
in a circlet on your dressing-table
(stone laid to stone)

still must somehow collect
some mirror, still reflect
a paler fold to its own diamond shape
folded so small.

The way I feel your feeling
at the last hour of your birthday
living in lowered lights
and seeing everything dance,

through the thong of grass binding
once intersecting winds —
(as if you were suddenly opposite,
and gave me the field of your hand).

The Wake Sofa

If your name did not appear so
on tombs and grocers' shops,
I could rethink your spade-pressed fields
into commonplace, uncultivated land again.
This sealed-up, cloud-darkened country
would not push its leaves into that unroofed
sea-lit room you whipped up without wine.

I have not spoken words with roots
since I saw you;
the light around my eyes
from your transparent grass
is the tightness around everyone's lips.
Though there was all last August
to be spoken to or let go
and the riper air blew shadows bowl-shaped,
it's over, this summer too.

The hedge of daily telephone calls, cut away,
till it was said by the painfully lengthened
garden: the blue and white mosaic,
where your knowing the news
seemed to get bluer, worn down
by the pure lip of the sea
to this perfectly smooth sky,
won't pitchfork me up into living again.

So very capable of dying, walking away
from your hard chair, a pilgrim from your flesh.
Though everyone is wayfaring,
you see ahead of yourself
like a handful of grain flung in a semi-circle,
a feeling that has been existing forever,
but hasn't returned, and isn't enough for you.

In the turn of your book a cloud
formed in my neck and laid my arm
on your shoulder like some twisted necklace.
The sea, as I go out of the door,
laps like a redness over the smoke-grey floor,
a river under a river, underflowing.

Your eyes fall into their own
midday weight; I rub their frail ache in.
You change by what I hear of you
into the dim fluid of a year,
but when tables are crowded with flowers,
and autumn deepens its flame again,
I will be fertilised only by your thinking it:

on a black-grained day,
when women open their cloaks in firelit houses,
scarcely burning, flinging out their fingers,
I shall see what it meant
when I said I dreamt
your bitter sail near morning in my throat.

Ceramic and Wood for Bronze

for Carolyn Mulholland

All the angles of the twigs
seemed such twilight gossip
in their impure purple:

why did the last blue inch,
when there was just enough roof to cover it,
suddenly point itself in a raincloud?

You draw your finger along the tablecloth
of gold leaves on your black dress
as if they were inhabiting an old shell,

and its slow, dark fruitful spring
makes a plaster cast of the moon
like no book that ever slid from me.

Its whites and silvers and greens,
its brushed hills and one thread-coloured
road, its stripes of snow,

rub out of the frail moon a strong one
like a book whose spine I have read
with only the skin of the eye.

Our hands touched over the steel
wedding-ring; in the spurt of a stone
falling we were separately submerged.

But the window with the round top,
the first in your glass 'contemporary' room,
shows the new window a square of flowers.

Still Life of Eggs

for Sylvia Kelly

You are almost kneeling, a diagonal shoreline
between two harbours, in the house-fostered darkness.
The tilt of your head reflects the arc
of the tablecloth, the curve of the sea.
And if the weather could fling its reds,
greens, blues, and purples across table-tops
(thought upon the unthinking) the blue might stay
a river or a lake, the fraying edges fog.
Like the beginning of a painting you have been
so watched: like an additional storey squeezed
into a steep roof, you freeze
the forever ripening shadows under
your eyebrows and neck into younger stone.
Contained, containing — perfectly alone.

Dante's Own Day

I wanted to hold him only as cotton
holds sweat, a sub-sea, birth-green river
of eggs in a private nest of smell.

The struggles of a series of intertwisted minds,
arranged by no mind, one on top of another,
in a growing ribbon of warmth.

Not to be lived in, a shell may need to be
too sturdy, stretching backward from the unwritten
part of angel, that unhealthy tissue
around the moment.

An acorn of a blind, denuded, unbegun,
unsheltered and unfinished, draws across a floor
on the mortal side of language,

a leaf detaching itself
from the narrative 'tree'
attempts to seal its meaning.

Then the voice that supplied the story
will be a character rounded-off outside it,
writing itself into those fumbling breaks
through which desire is completely trained:
bound in the bed like an account book.

Drawing in Red Chalk at a Death Sale

A thick and womblike knot in the curtain
(precisely the posed muscles of a carpenter)
unnaturally compressed a reign of brown:

as if the sky had melted slightly,
with its two selves being turned by a pitchfork,
a string of rubies dashed through
the dark pearl, mock pearl, and the real moonlight.

I miss a serious amount of silk
from my arm where it nestles unsaid
in the bend of the L or goes to stone-pierced water
between the ornamental lips of the fingers;

and quarrel every chilly plane of that
particular leaf whose autumn kinship
tangles the pure green thread out of my flesh.

Constable's 'Haywain'

The incised triangle,
the angle of the sciatic notch,
divides the month from the year
in my father's birthdate:
as bone becomes transparent
against the background of viaticum.

As yet his tomb is corpseless,
his absent body richer than life;
the grave goods, bracelets
of piano strings snapped by him;
the semi-quavered darkness to light
where amber forms and collects.

Only my I, my lost skinfold,
has disturbed the ground
with this sentence of speechlessness
as if I owned the willed
or invented death
high on its bed of extrovert papyrus:

to justly cheat my wife-giver
and wife-taker
of his islandlike afterworld,
his multi-sided water journey,
by the passionate polygamy
of four hands (ours) at one piano.

Field Heart

If I had dipped the tip of my finger
in water to cool your tongue,
you would have tasted salt off trees
forty miles from the sea.

Our voices in ordinary conversation
floated between farmhouses:
the pilot-light of a candle
burned in the open air
with no attempt to flicker.

Firmly-knit thatch
simply rested on the eaves
of its own permeable weight.
Slowly and steadily, the storm
that shared your name
reduced its current,
till every attentively incomprehending
tile of your skin
caught and flamed.

Nothing was to be seen through the closed lids
of your eventful dreaming,
the closed avenue of your new senses
beginning as absolute strangers
their ready-to-be-reaped, matured homecoming.

Through some friction with material substance,
like engaging a clutch, or intermeshing gears,
you turned the dew into something enchanted,
unbolted, a collapsible telescope,
a balloon untethered, a ball
from which the air has escaped.

You were now inside a lift
rising between two floors, no longer noticeable,
being whipped like the cork of a champagne bottle
out through a dark and narrow shaft
or rushing valley, into a higher frequency,
a faster vibration — into all the Irelands!

Bring your loosened soul near,
look through,
meet my day-consciousness
in the lawfulness of what is living:
return a different June to me —
once only, slide
until the union holds.

Black Note Study

Now you are my Northerner,
more first than first love.
Your eyes just show me the smoke
settling on roads open to you
only because they are pure offerings.
All the locks of that country
turn with that key.
Sound travels four times as fast there,
the mouth I have always felt as world
is itself already a fraction
in a family of sounds, a sleep nest
of frozen music, not into the winter.

Such a violent return
to your unfrozen self, it is still possible
to change the names of your addressless
villages. The bone structure
of your picture
has inverted its spinning shape
so it makes sense at any speed.
Like two halves of a nest,
our fingers lie so close together
they almost overlap
or as the body moves within clothing.
Though you have moved your entire hand
to a new starting-point, what I play
with my thumb you are playing
with your fifth finger.

I hear two voices without either
disturbing the other — four harmonies
where there was only one.
One voice spells out the same notes
as the other in reverse order.
One violinist starts at the end,

the other at the beginning,
the backward version fits perfectly
against the forward.

The gap between our hands is no wider
than the middle section of a ship,
which used to be sure of its sun,
or the soundpost joining an instrument
inside, knowing the sky by heart.
And it's nothing to do with proximity
on the keyboard, or the playing length
of the string, on my unaccompanied cello,
if a single chord is repeated over thirty times,
or a note of C- or E-ness
is tied over into that blank space,
held like an undeniable
gull-screech underhand.

The Finder has Become the Seeker

Sleep easy, supposed fatherhood,
resembling a flowerbed.
Though I extract you here and now
from the soil, open somehow
your newly opened leaves:
I like to breathe what ought to be.

You desire to exist through me;
I want to disappear exhausted in you.
We are things squeezed out, like lips,
not that which serves as coverings —
give me the strength to distinguish myself
from you, such ill-matched wings.

Night furs you, winter clothes you,
Homerically studded in your different planting.
You jangle the keys of the language
you are not using, your understanding
of sunlight is more language than that,
your outcast sounds scatter their fluid carpet.

Your mouth works beyond desolation and glass.
Your mask draws nearer to the other mask.
Your tongue, layered with air, presses a triple breath.
Your thinking fingers possess the acoustic earth:
oh do not heal, dip your travelling eye
the length of my so tightly conceived journey!

Elegy for an Irish Speaker

Numbered day,
night only just beginning,
be born very slowly, stay
with me, impossible to name.

Do I know you, Miss Death,
by your warrant, your heroine's head
pinned against my hero's shoulder?
The seraphim are as cold
to each other in Paradise:
and the room of a dying man
is open to everyone.
The knitting together of your two spines
is another woman
reminding of a wife, his life
surrounds you as a sun,
consumes your light.

Are you waiting to be fertilized,
dynamic death, by his dark company?
To be warmed in your wretched
overnight lodgings
by his kind words and small talk
and powerful movements?
He breaks away from your womb
to talk to me,
he speaks so with my consciousness
and not with words, he's in danger
of becoming a poetess.

Roaming root of multiple meanings,
he shouts himself out
in your narrow amphora,
your tasteless, because immortal, wine.
The instant of recognition

is unsweet to him, scarecrow word
sealed up, second half
of a poetic simile lost somewhere.

Most foreign and cherished reader,
I cannot live without
your trans-sense language,
the living furrow of your spoken words
that plough up time.
Instead of the real past
with its deep roots,
I have yesterday,
I have minutes when
you burn up the past
with your raspberry-coloured farewell
that shears the air. Bypassing
everything, even your frozen body,
with your full death, the no-road-back
of your speaking flesh.

The Aisling Hat

October — you took away my biography —
I am grateful to you, you offer me gifts
for which I have still no need.

I search for a lost, unknown song
in a street as long as a night,
stamped with my own surname.

A spy-glass at the end of it,
a cool tunnel crushed by binoculars
into your grandfather's house.

The elegant structure of the heart
is a net cast over everything in sight,
its lace design of perforations, truancy.

Over your face a cognac eagleskin
was tightly stretched, my cart-horse,
dray-horse, drew your heavy chariot

chasing after time you beat aloud
which had already vanished into overtones:
you were his co-discoverer, his museum,

his clock of coal, clock of limestone,
shale or schist, his mountain top
sculpted into a foal, his warm pitcher.

Even your least movement was connected
with the very composition of the soil,
you lived and died according to its laws.

Your Promethean head radiated
ash-blue quartz, your blue-black hair
some feathered, Paleolithic arrowhead,

set off the bold strokes of your ungainly
arms, created for handshakes, sliding
like the knight's move, to the side.

You were intoxicated like a woman
caressed with the lips alone
by the noise of your thousand breaths.

You felt nauseated, like a pregnant
woman, a rose inscribed in stone,
unread newspapers clattered in your hands.

Your horse-sweat was the poetry
of collective breathing, your urine-colour
the sense of the start of a race.

Your eyebrows arched like a composer's,
an accordion of wrinkles repaired
the fluids of your forehead, then drew apart.

Your powerful thorax gave velvet-
throated orders, there was a married charm
in your nuptial animation floating forward

to sow itself in the arid
frontier atmosphere. Your skin changed
to an absolute courtesy

but never ceased dreaming;
seeds of laughter pierced your chest
that now lies ensconced in the velvet.

Broken sign of the unbroken continuum,
you fused into a single thread,
time fed you with lightnings and downpours

so you rained hushing sounds,
while river air hovered over the room
and sucked in a crescent of the sea.

You sharpened yourself like a pencil
in the tender midwife of your shell,
in your geometric giddiness.

Your golden hands like hills
of tired rags stirred up the dust,
flushed horseman, streaked feldspar.

There was fire in your hands, blisters
on your palms as if you had been rowing,
heavy fire in your naked eyes

monkish in their furious, yellowish
glitter, still and sensual the shining
points of your equine eyes.

Twin wings unseverable
were those enormous eyes, legs of the heron
reconciled to their uselessness.

Neck of the swan theatrically
open, ripping off the days due to you,
expressing your allegiance.

A noose around the icy place
from which flowed your consciousness
like mineral-water cheeriness.

The earth like some great brown
ceiling came rushing at your head.
No one heard it hiss in the shadows.

Roses which must have been cut
in the morning stood exchanging lights,
as your phonetic light turned off

and the lips of your fireproof eye
burned like poppies, firmly reminding
everyone that speech is work.

Until we remembered that to speak
is to be forever on the road,
listening for the foreigner's footstep.

I felt a shiver of novelty
as if someone had summoned you
by name, to the most beautiful applause.

Your eye raised the picture
to its own level, you retreated
into the picture before my eyes

like hello or goodbye;
I got tangled up in it
as in a robe ready to be woven

from a soft *L* and a short aspiration,
or the most recent barbaric layer
the bark of linden peels off itself.

Woodcutting tuned you, absorptive
and resorptive, to an entire segmented
lemon grove of fatigue and secret energy.

You burst the frontier at some
undefended silk crack — shreds
of splashed brain on the chestnut trees.

Now all questions and answers rotate about —
did it thunder or not? Now I begin
the second stage of restoring the picture.

The helix of my ear takes on new whorls,
becomes a bittersweet instrument,
to undress spring from the neurotic May,

the inherited river, the world
which, unpopulated, continues
to signal his speech-preparatory moves.

He does not resemble a man
waiting for a rendezvous.
The area he covers in his stroll

is too large, he is still
a stranger there, until his storm matures,
and what might have been alive, knowledge-bearing.

His body is unwashed, his beard
wild, his fingernails broken,
his ears deaf from the silence.

Carefree skater on air, his language
cannot be worn down, though I
avoid it in my feebleness.

He controls my hair, my fingernails,
he swallows my saliva, so accustomed
is he to the thought that I am here.

I need to get to know his bones,
the deep sea origins of the mountains,
the capsule of his crypt,

how life below starts to play
with phosphorus and magnesium.
How cancelled benevolence gains a script

from a departure so in keeping
with its own structure — his denial
of history's death, by the birth of his storm.

PART TWO

Flirting with Saviours

It did not look as if anybody lived there,
rebellious sea on both sides of a narrow town.
Nature was a backdrop that had to be defended,
nothing could land at night, its night was so perfect.

Folded world of fierce under-winds that cried
eye-catching kisses most speakingly; basin
of enlaced hands, forensically linked
or fettered to the undecaying moon.

In our gentle meetings wrath did not seize them,
but the elements paused, without greatly moving air,
a kind of false or treasonable sunlight,
where something frightening that happened was fixed forever.

No nourishment other than chemicals.
Partly idyllic stoppage of time
that made the criminal fit the crime,
not rooted there but hazard-banished,
ruled out like the fear of being afraid.

Betrayers sent to guard, burnt wine,
outnumbered only by the one missing face;
outbreak of history better than no catastrophe ever.

Stored statelessness, hereafter glimpses,
surfaces to which gold could be applied, worse than saints —
men utterly outside themselves, with the taint of women.

Reverse Cinderella

I imagine your loverlessness,
how you kiss your own reflection in the glass.
In every street I see you,
making paths for my feet, my high shoes
laced with the widest ribbon.

My hat is broad as your shoulders,
my afternoonish dress long and loose
for lying down in.
I feel warmth coming from you
as clouds working up the sky
seen through warm clouds
that are cold at base.

The I you mean is the past walking in
to this place which is my enemy
and on your side — this strange level reach
of moorland held by magic above the sea.
Another I who is everybody
listens to your young voice
with my mature ear, the sound of rain
the moment after sunset.

You guide me like a cup
that might very easily break again
in the same place
through the table tombstone.
You are the first angry sign of life
growing jagged claws,
earning death as a way of living.

You don't mind if I leave you
to sit somewhere else, while you
lie dying, like my father speaking.

And like him I kissed you once
but you didn't know,
your face like a piano in the distance,
that only gaze, and its only return.

Black Virgin

Sea-black virgin — being in love with you
is a fine space. I will never live
in your searching wash, your grass wallpaper,
your bewildered red gardens.
You desire your wholeness, your virginity,
to be admired by angels only.
Such dry self-knowledge. Such sheer
Englishness — how could I
have mistaken you for my father?

For the old days when there used to be
people? Your days have a medieval structure,
your brief Cistercian night, with its night office,
has fought sleep always; for morning
you touch your lower eyelid, deep, awake,
healthy and wise and quiet, with your eyes clear.
What do you do with your eyes?

With your womb already primed
with its fern-like pattern, chasteberry,
chaste tree, monk's pepper?
If you are a woman there is no question
of a word like me being able to comprehend
the voice that uttered it, or its sign language
lordly and off-balance, with the inwardness
of war. Perhaps I am a sound
that was born with you, and finished
with you, your Lenten stomach
in a year when Easter was as late
as it could possibly be.

Or perhaps I am a military railway
to you, another city, with transient
miles of criminals. But when rain arrives
on the far side of emptiness,

like an identity scarcely dreamed,
and surrounds you with its unintelligible
silence, its enormously comforting speech —
even if it is talking to itself,
as long as it talks, I will listen.

The Colour Shop

1

Bereft of my flowers early in the season,
I found you condemned to spend whole seasons, alone.

Being half torn up by the storm, yet clinging
to the earth, I found the surge in you
more beautiful than the sea, because it waits
for man to inhabit it.

You were a midwinter of pleasures,
your man's life being a man's dream.

Bold-breasted and full of seeds,
wine-coloured lilacs in full bloom,
special drama of mobile light,
your mornings emerged out of the ground
rather than the sky.

Your branching lifted up
the sky's lilac whiteness, to spaces
more infinite, a journey of more balm
than the road I trudged.

Like a soul in a body
you could hardly bear
to be above ground, you had each other,
as the soul is a mirror before
painting it is a home;
or as two people walk side by side as
one, as perhaps lovers.

Broken, obsessed with twilight
as your favourite of all times,
you lay entombed in dark cells
like someone who stands in his own light.

You do not possess
what you need to be productive,
but my tenderness that isn't tender
enough floods in by every other post.

You have backs when one sees you
from the front, there is airiness
around you, though you are all tainted,
outside the paint, and every fold
is a denial, your deep-set eyes
say no, say little, and only
in the language of destination.

Upholding dogma, bringing an ice-axe
to yourself, you made my heart hot,
it was you who discovered the morning,
by the muscularity of your fields,
your sky knotted with clouds.

Border town without a slanting ceiling,
bench that waited for its occupant
with the tiredness and simplicity
of the person yet to arrive.

How did you, rough-barked men,
break into flower, with Death behind you
shaking his head, as behind a young couple?

Why was the lilac-black of your furrows,
your ever-rotting heather, accompanying someone
who is already dead, an enchanted territory
where one very quickly found oneself
up against a wall?

I encircle the very emptiness I feared
in the oasis bright and deep
where you live. And the bitter frost
that salvaged reality, with
or without permission, ended.

2

I was half-dead until the end of April,
unable to make sense of my mail
or the mental labour of balancing
six essential colours, a lullaby in colours,
with the old sense of cradling.

I needed your vital transfusions through the post,
I needed you to say something comforting,
as music is comforting, my audacious weddings
of colours, spring you must have felt
was being created yet again
out of yourself.

I know you only as one red,
one yellow, one blue. The absolute pole,
the final term in a series.
I regret your curly coat edges
and apple-green buttons are not alive.

But your night is more alive,
richer than my day,
your sheet and pillows very light, lemon-green,
though your face is drained to a pallor.
I still have your head, body, arms, legs,
all in my keeping.

For two months I have been permanently
drunk on your orchards, as on a street
of kind girls, as if I had been present
at a rebirth of all I should have believed in,
could have wished for.

You are cottages that share one thatch,
you sprout a double chimney,
though you are broken pitchers that have lost grip
on your memory in the prime of life.

You fear the onset of spring as you fear Christmas,
you are violet as the earth after rain,
you retrieve the betrayed North of my soul.

You part like a large beard, as if
you were my son or my brother;
I stick to you against your will
like pieces of field, the wary outline
of a child into which
the mother's profile could fit.

Your peaceful upright lines of young trees
have clearly left the human world,
the bankruptcy of worm-eaten states.

Powerful ruffians in the middle
of a room where one can ruin oneself,
go mad, commit a crime, I lean
back into you as into a gale,
the tiny lung-particles
of the world's virginity.

As if I had boarded a nineteenth-century
train at a quarter after midnight,
vibrating in the exciting blue
of 'real' love, wind along the landscape,
and the rest will slowly, slowly happen.

3

It was a menagerie. They seemed to think
they were at a resort of sea-green curtains
with a design of pale roses.
The street was being torn up, narrowly
avoiding its own disintegration,
their space was wonderfully traced with paths
to greet ghosts and join hands with the dead.

Their town was busily complete in itself
and insulated, they were people withdrawn
to a great distance from our dimmed
and troubled colours.

After the high yellow note,
it was better if he remained shut up
and thanked her for her letters' deliverance
that fell simply like strokes
of filtered rain, in blurry slants.

O dark fulfilment behind an obstacle,
my path to you is blocked by a stone fence.
In broad daylight with sun pure-gold,
you are a wildly tilted field enclosed
by a long, long wall of stone.

I see the irregular fenced ground
changing before my eyes — being reaped
to the delicate violet of a dug-up
and weeded piece of soil.

To the right the enormous available
sun radiates, love waits to one side
close to your heart but missing it.

You are helpless to advance into the world
and live there, broken-up sun
scattered in the wheat, objects in strain,
source of turmoil, clump of shapeless
disturbed trees and bushes, of birds
brushed by something like a halo.

You are being painted out,
but still you choose your side,
till I arrive almost smiling,
like a southern death.

The Over Mother

In the sealed hotel men are handled
as if they were furniture, and passion
exhausts itself at the mouth. Play kisses
stir the circuits of the underloved body
to an ever-resurrection, a never-had tenderness
that dies inside me.

My cleverly dead and vertical audience,
words fly out from your climate of unexpectation
in leaky, shallowised night letters —
what you has spoken?

I keep seeing birds
that could be you when you stretch out
like a syllable and look to me
as if I could give you wings.

Waxwing Winter

Often you may have the bird in full view
only for a few seconds,
an all-brown bird with dagger-like beak,
its scapulars lightly oiled from wading.

It lives much on the ground,
its wings outstretched
as if flying were hard work.

You must wear quiet clothing, for its ear
is completely under outer feathers,
as its ringed leg-bones reach
a long way into the body.

It bathes in smoke and windswept flight.
If it is found towards the end of the day
you must put its wing out of action
until it is healed or free
of flesh in a fume-cupboard.

Its heat is what for us would be fever:
if you use the fingers of one hand
to form a 'cage', can you hear
through the leaf litter and imagined open space
the light-proof birdsong
as the bird itself might hear it?

Skull-Light

Think of certain inexplicable deaths
as sullied translucent patches on sea,
the sky a stagnant pool. The river
of women wash down their walls
with milk of lime and household starch
for All Saints sideways on purpose now.

I make my Easter walking between the graves,
head high in the air, and seem to be losing him
twice over, though I am far more truly dead,
fastened like a limpet to this strip of land.

The real look is creeping back into his eyes,
eyes I feared to read, that nailed or burned
the words to my lips, and made of his death
with their sudden flaming up a perfect end.

That strange current he gave forth,
as though a beloved red from the topmost
part of evening, a scarce-born animal
in spices, that frozen light
too intense for even the smallest shadow —
what morning, like a sleeve too wide,
without costing much, can be breaking in me?

Credenza

A white melancholy sits in the lesser chair
at the front edge of time. In her moments
of cut radiance, colour runs all through her
like a hand-coloured paper Annunciation
in a gold-leaf frame. Then she has the sky-hook air
of here and there.

Not remembering him every day and every day
and every day has begun, the wet shoulders
of his breathing ending, the open rafters
of his inner nature little by little
never meeting again.

Her fingers explore the white keys only,
her fiery dress of tricolour ribbons
asks nothing from the low lights of the house,
where the piles of captured cannon
that had raised two pyramids
are being taken away.

Suddenly the all-black room sees everything
far down the street; war-talk sentences
act as if they had never been shot at;
a for-keeps winter inches wide
the voice of a wine the grapes
never belonged to.

The Albert Chain

Like an accomplished terrorist, the fruit hangs
from the end of a dead stem, under a tree
riddled with holes like a sieve. Breath smelling
of cinnamon retires into its dream to die there.
Fresh air blows in, morning breaks, then the mists
close in; a rivulet of burning air
pumps up the cinders from their roots,
but will not straighten in two radiant months
the twisted forest. Warm as a stable,
close to the surface of my mind,
the wild cat lies in the suppleness of life,
half-stripped of its skin, and in the square
beyond, a squirrel stoned to death
has come to rest on a lime tree.

I am going back into war, like a house
I knew when I was young: I am inside,
a thin sunshine, a night within a night,
getting used to the chalk and clay and bats
swarming in the roof. Like a dead man
attached to the soil which covers him,
I have fallen where no judgment can touch me,
its discoloured rubble has swallowed me up.
For ever and ever, I go back into myself:
I was born in little pieces, like specks of dust,
only an eye that looks in all directions can see me.
I am learning my country all over again,
how every inch of soil has been paid for
by the life of a man, the funerals of the poor.

I met someone I believed to be on the side
of the butchers, who said with tears, 'This
is too much.' I saw you nailed to a dry rock,
drawing after you under the earth the blue fringe
of the sea, and you cried out 'Don't move!'

as if you were already damned. You are muzzled
and muted, like a cannon improvised from an iron
pipe. You write to me generally at nightfall,
careful of your hands, bruised against bars:
already, in the prime of life, you belong
to the history of my country, incapable
in this summer of treason, of deliberate treason,
charming death away with the rhythm of your arm.

As if one part of you were coming to the rescue
of the other, across the highest part of the sky,
in your memory of the straight road flying past,
I uncovered your feet as a small refuge,
damp as winter kisses in the street,
or frost-voluptuous cider over
a fire of cuttings from the vine.
Whoever goes near you is isolated
by a double row of candles. I could escape
from any other prison but my own
unjust pursuit of justice
that turns one sort of poetry into another.

The Radio Traitor

Last year's honey, ill-preserved, bitter beyond
all sweetening, is set down at another point
in aridity, but drawn here by your longing.

One of time's gables runs back to simplicity
in your jessamined window. Because you offended
the root of the law, your halls, stairs and passages
are in perpetual dusk. Because you rejoiced
in the thought of the English dead lying under
the West Wall, you were always treated
as British, whether you were or not.

Men and men and men crowd at a stretch of water
washing their clothes, with vague faces,
with defined bodies, all different phases
of the same man. You open and shut
your breast, the rudiments of musketry,
bayonet fighting, squad drill. Blood leaves
your hands, your feet, your limbs, and flows
back to your heart like a cold change in the room.

Waking opposite your neckfires, my pushed mind
slept. You stepped faster than spring, defeating
that love that swears itself undying,
taking the sky's enamelwork with you,
being pearly above, where the rain falls.

The Nearness of the Grape Arbour
to the Fruit Cellar

Like an open prayer book against a body,
two roads cross exactly on that corner.
So it seems like an end but is not,
as marriage is not.

He was not a country but the material
out of which countries are made.
He was lying in long loose waves
of broken land;
I had never seen any blood so bright,
so frozen hard enough not to smell.

The gash was torn from inside, outward;
he felt his way through lilacs, trickling
them through his fingers, as if he were separating
hair, its mere shadings in grass.

His features might have been cut out of a shell
they were so transparent.
His chest like a young blacksmith's
arched his shoulders, now brown and in seed,
so the country seemed
to lift itself up to me and come very near,
with the dried stalks, the dead stand, of last year.

His hands, burned red, looked calm, but blazed
with the things he could not say,
the other side of the pattern
that is supposed not to count.

His earth-owl eyes warmed the guttered
slope of my back with their swift fires,

such vivid pictures, they might have been
his memories, but promised
new things for living people.

A silence seemed to ooze out of the ground:
he coupled his mellow thunder to it
as a work-horse to its yoke-mate,
as if he knew it was to piece him out
and make a whole creature of him.

So with a pull that brought curling muscles
to the smooth, sun-warmed hips of the horses,
he cut his body loose from the pool
of field dust scarcely larger than the bed that held him,
a sleeve hanging empty, a good
tight box that would turn water.

Yet never scattered his beads
nor raised his hands except to cross himself,
till I was left alone with the older voice
of a winter which lies too long,
has overslept, or early awakened,
enjoys the deepening grey.

Between the 8 and the 9

O Provins rose, world as wanted,
you were for touching, soft as mohair:
your fragrance after rain or being touched
contrasted with the feel of trees.

Dramatic leaf-shape in reflective water,
a kind of shimmering in space,
a sort of vortex, completely dark,
with a rim of some description . . . .

You had no tendency to fade
like a dream, though when I try
to touch you, my hand goes through you,
like a wished-for body, or the bones

of a garden. Your strong colour
with its harsh red temperature
acted like punctuation. Your day
scent was the scent of decay.

Now if I rub you with snow
and think you quiet, I only dream
the pattern of your hunting magic,
not the sleep of the snows.

Your wintersweet heart was a loveless
thread, your art the art of strewing;
and your last body is not far in
when we discover your next glorious body.

The War Degree

You smell of time as a Bible smells of thumbs,
a bank of earth alive with mahogany-coloured
flowers — not time elaborately thrown away,
(you wound yourself so thoroughly into life),
but time outside of time, new pain, new secret,
that I must re-fall in love with the shadow
of your soul, drumming at the back of my skull.

Tonight, when the treaty moves all tongues,
I want to take the night out of you,
the sweet Irish tongue in which
death spoke and happiness wrote:

a wartime, heart-stained autumn drove
fierce half-bricks into the hedges; tree-muffled
streets vanished in the lack of news.
Like a transfusion made direct from arm
to arm, birds call uselessly to each other
in the sub-acid, wintry present. The pursed-up
fragrances of self-fertile herbs
hug defeat like a very future lover.

Now it is my name and not my number
that is nobody now, walking on a demolished
floor, where dreams have no moral.
And the door-kiss is night meeting night.

Timed Chess

You break the darkness like an apple,
making fingers of lips and lips of fingers.
You twist leathered wrists into hands,
fold mortal messages in the slow closing
of both eyes, till only the face counts.

Sometimes, like an old piece of the coast,
following in cloud pieces the shapes
of Italian clouds, you send a strange
perfume in your stead, indubitably male,
a carnation passed through a button-hole.

No journey is more safely beautiful
than all the miles of you, your many
degrees of death lying almost a lifetime
in the distance. When the sky turns frail
over your many-lobed harbour, your
sea-quality opens fresh petals.

Your hedges hesitate to change,
keeping their beard like an over-hanging war
or a slightly cowardly peace.
Your sun-hungry, end-of-winter colours
incompletely shed the enemy world.

The denier of my sleep, woman-or-ghost,
is a full river; looted wines
in large throatfuls flavour the tight
air; all the land is behind, the unworked
nowhere, repeating the her and the her.

Captain Lavender

Night-hours. The edge of a fuller moon
waits among the interlocking patterns
of a flier's sky.

Sperm names, ovum names, push inside
each other. We are half-taught
our real names, from other lives.

Emphasise your eyes. Be my flare-
path, my uncold begetter,
my air-minded bird-sense.

For the Wind Millionaire

There is no point escaping from the world
unless everyone knows you have escaped
and taken from it all that you wished —
high walls, pedestrian zones,
darker than white pigeons:

the memory of a memory looped
through the spare shutters;
it came from below as from theatre footlights,
into a perfumed ghetto,
its guerrilla action scenting your art:

the invented part
of your life so free of secrets,
a picture of you from mid-thigh upwards
like a bullet upended on my desk.

Your slow-igniting cigarettes,
your wind-bleached hair just felt
as it dulls the skin, and no more.
Your bruised hands tightly pressed
against the seams of your trousers,

your abused head, your knotted,
fragile face, your laugh taped
like a very deep harbour, two winters
before the year before last.

It had a meaningless tenderness,
it was your gospel self,
your North Britain nightmares
about the first German you killed,
how you did not stop except to change
your bloody shirt . . . .

Ours is a true city, meanly built,
in sharper weather my roof leaks
around the nine bomb-holes.
We were all born blinking
at the alien glitter
of an artificial moon.

Our criminals are like the sun;
part of the pseudo-royal decor,
the inflammable underbrush that sells
and re-sells, they cover wounds
like the sun.

As parts they do not make a whole
except in strangers' eyes.
Their part-songs slow the ripening
of something which it takes a man
twenty years to say.

Gardens made to be seen close-up,
made to be admired from indoors,
they are destined to die of the war
twenty-five years after the Armistice
when the land, stale from leftover seasons,
was ready, and the sea,
for the first time, restoring:

our new view of the sea as fertile
turned us peasant with the season;
we carried the dead uncovered
through the streets, and fixed
who the new people would be
in their discarded graveclothes,

their new names running
through the country like a train
and ignoring it — the laws after all
having been imported —

a place without politics, firmly run,
by flowers in suitcases with mustn't-grumble
voices . . . . Rusting there is second-best
to dreaming of the membrane of your mouth.

Apostle of Violence

There is an extra gathering of snow
over the prisoner on the Roman triumphal arch:
his arms are bare, his legs crossed,
his lips wind-packed with snow, not twisted
in pain, his sixteenth-century eyes
are used all the more
breaking their snow-lids to the outer morning.

Windows higher on the outside
than on the inside lead his eyes upwards
to tabernacle corners, blind-windows belonging
in the ceiling's world.
A blend of morning's freshest hours
blows through his wind-clothes
till his right hand seems a brother by his side.

The rivers that are the companions
of the times of the day
reply with the gift of a day in his life
in the person of night,
a day too heavy for one angel,
like an empty throne, at the stair-foot door,
open the length of the ice-veiled garden.

White Windsor Soap

In the hospital robe of your Catholic eyes,
their bars painted prison-issue blue,
like a submarine, I have been
entirely released.

Their weather, life and spousehead stand
at a forty-five degree slope
in encased bridges, but you flow
to me as fresh air or the lost
sensation of rain, I read and read
the tiny names you talk to.

In a world of no strangers, nothing
can be exchanged except words.
From three double-layered one-way
windows along, I hear you
being opened up, a source of sounds,
waving like a snake's back.

I was going to add this blood
to the blood embedded in the tiles,
the headlock of your thoughts
as you sat there all that time,
so scared by deep lungfuls of you.

Dividing the Political Temperature

Like two stones in Tuscan water, we intersect
without meeting, without the water breaking;
its little wounds open and close like a mouth
to feed, over a furrowed throat; like a transparent
vase into the single deep black: like the opposite
of water. Stars twinkle as if in my womb,
their endless ribbon brushes the weak erection
of dreamlets, its rhythm swallowed only
by the shapeless wall — could we be
more cruel to one another, virgin recalling
virgin, not the flesh of your flesh,
a door planned behind your shoulder,
using the earth to live in, not being
the time-being earth?

How like death, and unlike death,
the reeds and silk of your kiss, rendered
unrecognisable by death, that struck me
free of all sunlight on the cusp
of the lips, in the grace of the shadows,
the wafer of your mouth, the body of
your mouth, your body's mouth, your mouth's
body. So we became a double tomb
when they collected the dead at dusk,
so one soul governed our two bodies.
Cobbled double-storm beach made
of ill-assorted thirst and sleep strikes.
Why did the weather not take me with it,
close friend of spring, that almost
Parisian feel that comes and goes?

I explore your seabed like a knife embedded
in a table, you are fragile as paper or fossilised
seaweed, the tree of your veins like lilies
caked in silver. One bell produces the effect

of four. I see the moon enlarged in a dazzling stain
whose spiral pains your held-awake eyes.
Your head is a Mediterranean echo of self,
a mirror-script of loanwords I can finger
into small rooms. The woven image of your face
covers my bedsheet, placed under strong torsion:
wineskin full of dust, your arms the drawbridge
taste of innocence; nothing will now disturb our night.